Interrupted My Redeemed Life
A Memoir

Empris V. Jones

Life Notes Publishing
www.LuvandNumbers.com

Interrupted: My Redeemcd Life, A Memoir
Published by Life Notes Publishing
Written by Empris V. Jones

Cover design by Tonya M. Chandler
Scripture quotations marked NIV are taken from the Holy Bible, New International Version ®, NIV ®. Copyright ©1973, 1978, 1984, 2011 by Biblica, Inc. ® Used by permission of Zondervan. All rights reserved worldwide. www.zondervan.com. The "NIV" and New International Version" are trademarks registered in the United States Patent and Trademark Office by Biblica, Inc.®

Scripture quotations marked NKJV are taken from the New King James Version®. Copyright ©1982 by Thomas Nelson. Used by permission. All rights reserved.

A few select verses are paraphrased by the author.
This memoir is a truthful recollection of actual events in the author's life. The names of individuals have been changed to respect their
privacy.

Dedication

to my son (first breath 2005-last breath 2008)
and my daughter. I deeply love the two of you with everything in me. In
heaven and earth, you both are my world!

to my readers and all those who struggle with same sex attraction, I
hope my life inspires you to run after God and encounter Him like never
before. He is the mender of broken hearts!

contents

Acknowledgements

the Only True Living God, My Father! Thank you for interrupting the plans of the enemy over my life and getting me to this place in You. I Love You, Lord!

the late Bishop Billy K. Bamberg (1953-2015) and Apostle Rodney Cain, thank you from the bottom of my heart for being there for me. My life was in a difficult situation when I came to LCOM. Thank you for loving me with the love of Christ as your spiritual daughter and pushing me to be who God called me to be.

my editor, my dearest friend, Loretta, thank you for your prayers and the gift God has blessed you with to be a blessing to me in editing this book. There will be many more, I'm going to have to get my bread up, Lol!

Introduction

My Life was Broken!

The innocence of a young girl was interrupted to the point of confusion, should she be with a man or a woman. She chose both. Perversion whispered in the ear of a young boy who violated the innocence of a young girl; that young girl was me, Empris V. Jones. As I put words to paper, I unveil the events that caused my life to spiral out of control. Conversations about same sex attraction is more than political, social, or taboo, it's personal. It is the outward expression of broken hearts, wounded souls, and mistaken identities.

Every person has a life story that led them to brokenness or to wholeness. My brokenness led me to Redemption...Jesus Christ! I surrendered my life to God. When I ignorantly pursued what I thought was love and acceptance, God kept me! Just like the woman at the well (John 4: 29), He knew everything about me!

In my own voice, I share with you, Interrupted My Redeemed Life, a Memoir. I take you on my journey of a broken heart that blossomed into a Redeemed Heart!

Empris V. Jones
Warner Robins, GA
2024

From Interruption to Redemption

Chapter 1

In the Beginning

February twenty-fifth. Nineteen eighty-five. West Palm Beach, Florida…my life began. I was born at a strong six pounds and one ounce to my mother. She was alone during my birth, but being alone did not stop her joy. My mother was ecstatic about me!

My mom had no idea who my dad was and the guy who she thought was my dad was not. When she saw the deep pools in my cheeks, it was then she realized who my dad was. My mom said I was a beautiful, bright-eyed, round -faced baby with dark brown skin. My dad was at work the day I was born. My family told him the news of my birth, but he didn't have any clue as to which hospital I was born in. I grew up living with my mom who eventually had my siblings. In my child's mind, I was not too happy about the addition to our family. But as I experienced the challenges of an interrupted life, my siblings were my constant companions.

They were my partners in war, born to soften the hardness of adversity. My mom and dad were never married. Separately they both had five children each. My father had a child who died prematurely, at least that is what I heard.

I could remember a few great moments from my childhood; childlike moments of purity, innocence, and simplicity. My siblings and I played in dirt piles near the train tracks when we lived in Riviera Beach. Playing in those dirt piles was the calm before the storms. Before the chaos, life was fun.

If I could describe my childhood in one word, I would say it was stressful. My partners in war and I dealt with a lot growing up. My family was not wealthy. We did not have a lot of money. My mother worked, received child support and governmental assistance to take care of us. I remember eating block cheese and nasty, watery peanut butter; I hated that peanut butter. I would cry when I had to eat it because it was hard and not smooth like store- bought peanut butter. It was disgusting!

Every summer we would go to my grandmother's house in Boynton. It was fun! Grandma was our reprieve. She was like cool water in the desert. Grandma was oxygen in our lungs. She took us with her to run errands, to shop for groceries and to church. The food she cooked was good for our bodies and our souls. She did our hair: ponytails, braids and haircuts for my brother.

Empris V. Jones

Easter Sunday 1997, I was so beautiful! My grandma candy curled my hair. We were dressed to impress, my siblings and me! Grandma was our sure foundation when life was not so sure.

Chapter 2

It Started in the Dark

As a child, I remember things always happening to me. I was accident prone: my hand got cut, I was burned with an iron, and I almost drowned in the pool. However, there was one incident that changed my life tremendously. I remember walking from our three- bedroom apartment in Rivera Beach off J Avenue to my mother's friend's apartment. My mother's friend had two daughters and a son. I was in kindergarten...five years old.

As I was going up the stairs to their apartment, I was greeted at the door by the daughters. When it was time to go to bed, I recalled going into the son's bedroom. In the middle of the room was a dark mahogany bunk bed. I was told to sleep on the bottom bunk. He, the son, and I were in the same room, but he was on the top bunk plotting to do the unthinkable.

When the lights were off, and the door closed…baby, baby it was another story. I did not have a clue about what it was about to happen, but what happened to me that night, happened to my entire life. I was lying on the bed trying to go to sleep when he called me to the top bunk. He then told me to get on top of him. I did as I was told. I did not understand what was happening, but most of all, I did not like it. He continued by fondling me and had me rubbing up against him.

After that encounter, I did not tell anyone what happened. I was just glad to be going home across the street. I was home, but I was changed, I was not the same. Something happened to me…I was opened and exposed. Seeds of sexual perversion were sown in my soul. I did not know it then, but those seeds were sure to bear fruit…strange fruit.

I attracted undesired attention from the little boys at my school. I did not know what to do with such attention. I remember when I was in the first grade sitting at a table with my teacher and other students, the boy who was sitting next to me had his hand in my pants touching me. Growing up, even close male relatives tried to get at me in this same way. I could not understand what it was about me. Boys were all over me like hound dogs. Did they know something I didn't know?

Chapter 3

Where are the Good Men?

Our childhood was challenging. We had to grow up fast, adjusting to new schools, new areas, and new friends each time we moved. Children are resilient, but the episodes of my life tested and stretched wide the boundaries of my childhood sanity. Moving from place to place with my mother and siblings became a constant and unnerving task. Each move signaled my mother's relationship with a new man. In all honesty, I wished it were just us and not those men in our home. Our dads did not live with us. I did not remember them growing up, but I remembered the men my mom married or dated. They did not have wedding ceremonies, so I guess most of the marriages were officiated through the court. They were not good men. Those men added chaos to our lives.

As a child, I did not have the words to say how I felt. But as an adult, I can now say I felt lost, uprooted, and unprotected. I thought good men were supposed to cover, protect and care for their loved ones, but that was not our experience. Where were the good men? I could remember the time we fought off the first man my mother married. He was a crackhead. He broke into our house and stole our stuff. Even worst, this man would fight our momma. One day, he snuck in through the back door which led to the kitchen. We had something for him. We put pots and pans to his behind that day! Every lick was in defense of our momma. Though we had challenges, as a family, we were close- knitted. We loved, covered, and defended each other.

Out of my mother's five husbands, one of her husbands was okay. He was a white man, a little weird, but he was ok. Then there was another husband who would always get on my case about something. I could not stand him, and he felt the same way about me. I was so stressed with him in the house, I developed shingles. Then there was the nice Jamaican guy. I do not know what happened to him. I liked him. He ironed our clothes. We never knew his name, so we called him Tailor because he was a tailor by profession.

My dad came by at times, but he did not come to visit me. He came to visit my mother, if you know what I mean? I was grown and on my own when my mother met and married her last husband. I did not see positive examples of men growing up. I saw lust, unbridled desires and fornication. I must confess, as an adult the same behaviors that caused chaos in my childhood became a mainstay in my own life.

Chapter 4

The Kiss

In my freshman year of high school, I met a nice guy who I liked. I thought he was handsome. He, however, had a best friend who was also after me, but all the best friend wanted to do was kiss and have sex. I was not feeling the sex part. I did not know why, but I wasn't ready for all of that just yet; my focus was mainly on school. Plus, my mom would have killed me if I dated, liked, or even talked to any boys. In my teen years, unwanted attraction and behaviors followed me. I became a slave to it. Unconsciously, I was looking for authentic love, but I was attracting chaos disguised as love.

A small fire of curiosity was starting to burn in my soul. Not liking it or knowing what to do about it, the fire continued to burn. During my sophomore year of high school, things got real. There was a girl, an immature eleventh grader, who did things to get my attention. For instance, throwing pennies at me as I walked to my gym class.

I could hear clinging every now and then in the distance, but I never felt a thing. Later, she told me she was throwing pennies at me to get my attention. I was not impressed, nor did I think it was funny or cute. We made it to the gym to get changed for track. Somehow, I was left alone with her in the dressing room. She kissed me. I didn't know what to do at first, so I slapped her in the face because I knew it was not right. Although I was called gay when I was younger, I never had anything happen to me like this. I never did anything to anyone to show I was gay. I did not hear much about what it meant to be gay until my sophomore year of high school.

In that moment, I was vulnerable and confused. I kissed her back. It was wrong, but I liked it. We began dating…love letters, walks to class and gifts were a part of our dating relationship. It was like puppy love. Whatever that meant! In school, I was considered a full-blown lesbian, a fem, a term for a feminine lesbian. At that point, I didn't care what anyone had to say. I was turned out by her, a term used in the gay community for your first encounter with someone of the same sex. Eventually the puppy love died down and we broke up, but we kept in touch and remained friends. However, my first gay encounter opened the door to the gay lifestyle which included clubbing in gay clubs, fighting and serial dating. My relationship with God, my upbringing and what I learned in church faded into the background of my new life. My life was Interrupted!

Chapter 5

Catchin' Feelins'

It was one day after track practice; I went to my friend Christine's house. Her older brother answered the door standing 6"1, light brown skin, medium built, with his manhood sticking out of his pants. I just asked for my friend and walked into her room thinking nothing of it, not even a mention of what I saw.

We all started to hang out and go to the movies, Christine, her brother, and my best friend. I guess someone started to have feelings for me. Christine's brother Anthony started gathering information about me. He found out I was gay, a lesbian, but that did not deter him, go figure. This was the first of many red flags dealing with Anthony, but eventually we started dating. He was nice, and wasn't all over me like the other guys, so I decided to give him a chance. What he didn't know, he was not the only person I was dating. In school, I had a girlfriend who I saw

My family had their speculations, but never said anything to me about being gay. To this day, I do not know what their silence meant. Maybe they did not know how to deal with my gayness, my same sex attraction. Maybe it was too new and unfamiliar to my family. During my senior year of high school, Anthony and I moved in together. Our home was a little shabby, one bedroom, one bath house beside his mom's friend's house. They let us rent the place; or at least I thought they did. I had no idea. I was still in school, and I did not have a real job. I helped my uncle with his lawn-care service as his secretary, entering data into the computer for his invoices. However, I did not get much pay, just enough to go shopping sometimes.

Graduation time arrived. I went to all my senior events… grad night, prom, etc. Anthony was my prom date. It was a fun evening. After graduation, I was ready to go to college and enjoy a new level of freedom. I completed my financial aid forms (FASFA) with the help of my favorite teacher.

Though I was distracted by the events of my life, I was a good student and maintained good grades. I applied to the colleges of my choice. Florida State University was my first choice among other colleges. I eagerly waited to receive acceptance letters, but I did not receive any. Not because I was not accepted, my applications were not mailed. I believed I missed my opportunities because of jealousy and sabotage. When I applied to Florida Memorial in Miami, I asked Anthony to mail the application. I trusted him to do as I asked.

Whether it was irresponsibility or sabotage, my application was never mailed. I found my application in his mother's room while looking for his belongings. I was hurt and disappointed. So, I put off college for a while trying to work and play house with Anthony.

Chapter 6

Tumbleweed, Unstable

I have always been a go-getter. In 2005, I saved my money and gathered up money from my grandma for a two-bedroom apartment. The apartment was in Rivera Beach at the Wedgewood Plaza Complex. The lease was in my name and my best friend Christine's name. The apartment was very nice and spacious. Renting the apartment was a rite of passage into adulthood! A few months into our relationship, Anthony and I were pregnant. It was early in my pregnancy when the doctors discovered my baby did not have a heartbeat.

The doctors performed an emergency D and C to remove my lifeless baby from my body. I was devastated, I didn't know if it was a boy or girl. I didn't get to see his or her beautiful little face, he or she was just gone. I cried my eyes out. Anthony's way of helping with the situation was to take me out to eat at Denny's. Nothing on Denny's menu could heal the pain in my heart. Not only was I mourning the loss of our child, but I was also angry with Anthony. My heart was broken!

Eventually with all the sexing, Anthony and I were pregnant again. I was happy about the pregnancy. I took pictures of each stage of my pregnancy. I went full term and then some. I was still dating women which was a part of the reason Anthony, and I were going through tough times, arguing, and fighting. He wanted to control me, and I refused to be controlled by him. The more he tried to control me, the more I wanted to be with someone who would console me and not control me.

My girlfriend at the time was Nicky. I met her at a club called Jay's in Fort Lauderdale. We spent a lot of our time clubbing and hanging out. Nicky was the bomb at what she did. She was I'd say 5"6, light skin with dreads, heavy set 230 pounds and masculine in all her ways. She was a true stud (masculine female). I loved Nicky with everything in me or I loved the sex or just both. She treated me like a queen. However, Nicky was not up for any foolishness. I couldn't be back and forth with her and a dude; I had to be all in or not!

When Nicky found out I was pregnant, she took good care of me. She would rub my stomach and waited on me hand and foot. But she did not want me to hang out. I believe she had ulterior motives. For some reason, I did not trust Nicky. I believed she was trying to see other females while she was with me, especially her ex-girlfriend. They had an emotional bond I chose not to compete with. Nicky and I went our separate ways.

I bounced around like a tumble weed with Anthony until it was time to have the baby. I gave birth to a handsome baby boy. You could hear me down the halls of the hospital screaming, "Oh God, Oh God!" They kept telling me to push. I did as the midwife instructed as my baby born came into the world. There were some complications as the umbilical cord was wrapped around his neck. My baby was blue due to a lack of oxygen. I didn't know this, but my family told me later. When the doctors got him breathing, he was fine. My sweet boy was a cute, little bright skin scribbled up thing. He was in my womb too long. Anthony Jr. was 7 pounds 1 ounce. He was my sweet baby boy. Anthony along with our mothers, my cousin Julie, and my auntie Star were at Anthony, Jr's birth.

After three or four days, I was released from the hospital with Anthony Jr. in tow. Anthony was at my side. I went back to my mom's house because that's where we were living. Living with my mom was okay for a while, but I knew in my heart I wanted more. I wanted more out of life; a larger place I could call my own and money to afford the things I needed and wanted. I was tired of living with Anthony, jumping from place to place. Just as I was tired of Anthony, he was tired of my lesbian lifestyle. Our relationship was rocky. Anthony was very abusive; all he wanted to do was fight and sex me up when he felt like it. I was tired of going through the same cycles with him. I needed a break from Anthony and West Palm Beach. So, I decided little Anthony and I would move to Tallahassee for a new start and to attend college.

My life was unstable, but the desire of getting a college education was constant. It's safe to say, I never met a stranger. I made instant friends or maybe I attracted those who were like me in some way.

I met Jasmine. She was Tallahassee bound, and I joined her. Jasmine had her own place. Little Anthony and I stayed with her. Jasmine was different, a country girl from Texas. She was very nice and caring. Jasmine made sure Anthony, Jr., and I were okay. At the time, Anthony Jr. was two years old. My sweet boy was healthy, full of joy and thriving! He was my peace in the storm. I was uncertain about a lot of things in my life, but I was certain about my love for Anthony, Jr.

I attended Tallahassee Community College. I enjoyed the nightlife: clubbing and house parties were added to my list of things to do. Tallahassee was a college town; college students were everywhere. While I was there, I experienced things I never thought I'd do or even knew about. The thing I'm speaking of was orgies. I engaged in orgies with other lesbians. They were friends of my girlfriend at the time. I was considered an aggressive fem (the more dominant female) especially if I was in a lesbian, fem and fem relationship. When Jasmine and I got into it, I went back to Anthony. I did not want to be in a relationship with Anthony, but he was always around, accessible. He was familiar to me. He was my rescue for all the wrong reasons. Our relationship was toxic with negative cycles of fighting and sexing (sexual relations). Shortly thereafter, I was pregnant with my second child.

Pregnancy did not stop me from clubbing. My clubbing game was amplified. I was meeting women left and right. I moved in with another young lady; I liked her swag (her style). After we broke things off for reasons I don't remember, I moved in with another girl who I knew from West Palm Beach. I was so unstable. Every relationship I pursued was rocky. This relationship was no different than the other relationships. We were together, then we were not together.

As the days and months passed, it was time to give birth to my baby girl. She was born in Tallahassee Community Hospital. Her God Daddy was with me during her birth. Despite my chaotic personal life, I maintained good grades.

I missed my final exams as I gave birth to my daughter, but I passed all my classes. My season in Tallahassee ended. It was time to move back home to West Palm Beach and pick up the pieces of my life. I moved in with my auntie. I immediately began working at Wendy's, and a check cashing place. Working at the check cashing place ended quickly. My auntie got me a job at Savannah Court as a receptionist and then as a janitor so I could work full-time. Eventually, I was able to afford my own apartment. I was a working mother of two children, and a college student while continuing my extracurricular activities of dancing, meeting people, and hanging out at Cashmere, a gay club.

Chapter 7

That Day

On my way to work, I kept leaving things at home and having to turn around. This one day was different from any other day. I did not know it then, but something was going to take place that would again interrupt my life. I dropped the children off at my auntie's house to babysit them while I was at work. Anthony would have been my first choice to take care of the children, but he and I were no longer together. Our relationship was toxic. It was best for us to go our separate ways. He was no longer in my life.

I adhere to the pledge that true motherhood is sacrificial responsibility for her children. In other words, I did what I had to do. My job was down the street from my Auntie's house. Normally, I would call to check on the children when I arrived at work, but that day, I did not have a chance to call. I felt they were ok. I was only working a few hours a day.

As I was leaving work, I got a phone call from someone telling me my mom was in the hospital. Soon after that phone call, I got another call from one of my sisters telling me I needed to get to my auntie's house quickly. I did not know what was going on, but I rushed to my auntie's house. There were police cars and an ambulance in the yard. Nobody would let me in the house. I did not know what happened. Then I saw the EMTs coming of out the house with my baby, Anthony, Jr. on a stretcher. I lost all composure! I started screaming. My auntie's house was on a hill. I jumped from the hill trying to get to my son. I can't recall if they told me what happened or how I knew, but my baby had been shot in the head. There were so many thoughts racing through my mind.

At the hospital, my son was pronounced dead. As I walked back to the lobby in shock, all I could hear was Anthony's family saying things like, "let's get Layla before they shoot her like they did Jr." The hospital was in an uproar between my family and his family. I never saw my baby. I waited outside of the hospital so I could go back in later to see my baby before they took him, but the hospital said it didn't work that way. I left the hospital. My grief was so heavy, I went into a deep depression. I didn't know it at the time, but I was clinically depressed.

I did not have an appetite. I did not want to do anything, but just stay in bed. I didn't know what to do with myself. People were bringing me food. My girlfriend Valerie tried to help, but her help and attention wasn't what I wanted. I ended the relationship with her. I loved her and cared for her, but I was just depressed.

At this point, I had totally given up on Anthony. I wanted to take the lesbian lifestyle to the next level. I remember us having parties for no special reason. I was trying to be sane. Then I met up with an old fling, Nicky. We tried to rekindle what we had, but after a while I got jealous. Nicky couldn't take me going through her phone, so we ended the relationship.

I started going to the club again trying to pick up the pieces of my life after the loss of little Anthony. I was trying to hold on to my sanity. Losing Anthony, Jr., was the hardest thing that I ever had to experience. At the club, I met Stacey, a brown-skinned stud with long dreads, heavy-set. She was nice. We first started kicking it and hanging out, trying to get to know each other. Stacey was different. She was smart and kind. Stacy had a sweet heart. I knew she wasn't trying to get close to me for any reason other than to be with me and to love me. Stacey loved me and I loved her back. Our relationship became serious. I asked her to live with me and my daughter Layla.

At that time, my best friend was still living with me. Everything was great! We hung out. We drank and did things couples do. Eventually, my best friend moved out. She got her own place. My best friend started to dislike Stacey. We didn't see eye to eye on some things. So, it was just the three of us; my daughter, Stacey and me, Empris.

Chapter 8

Mental Hospital

One day as I was going to work, something changed in my mind. I was forgetful. I did not know the day or time. This was the first sign something was wrong in my mind. My soul was grieving deeply and suffocating. My mind was drowning in sadness, shock, dismay and unanswered questions. Several months earlier, I lost Anthony, Jr. He was not lost in a store or playing hide and go seek lost. He was gone, never to be seen again in the earth. He was in heaven, yes, but my soul was sad, lonely and missing him. It was too much for my humanness.

I remember drinking an entire 5-hour energy drink to stay awake because I was working as a security officer. After work, I was asked to take Stacy's brother home. I was so turnt (term used for excited or extremely happy), I was going higher than normal. I was in a state of manic.

My friend Stacy was so scared I was going to hurt myself or someone else, she called a couple of her friends who were Christians to pray for me. As they prayed, I was going in and out of consciousness. I was blacking out. I did not understand what was going on, but the one thing I remembered was the Christian friends saying I needed to be delivered…whatever that meant. At this point in my life, I was so far from God. I did not know what was happening to my life. Too many bad memories in Boynton… I moved from my spacious three-bedroom apartment to Stacey's mother's house.

After the move, I continued to act strange and out of sorts. They attempted to give me a sleeping pill in my drink to calm me down, but something in me knew my drink was laced. I did not drink it. My manic behavior skyrocketed. I was Baker Acted (Florida Mental Health Act) and admitted to the hospital for mental evaluation.

Chapter 9

Encounter with Christ

While I was in the hospital, Stacy kept in contact with me. She came to visit on a regular basis. Stacy made sure I had everything I needed, but my emotional and mental state started having a draining effect on her, therefore, she had to take a step back. I was in and out of the hospital, either the medication was not agreeing with me, or I was misplacing the medication.

Eventually, I had another episode. Scared and alone, I walked barefoot down Congress Avenue in Boynton Beach. I was trying to get to the mental hospital. All I could see was holographic images of the things Jesus Christ went through as He died on the cross. Stacy called the hotline for mental emergencies. The police found me in the median. In route to the mental hospital, I was going in and out of consciousness, but I was calling on Jesus. I thought the mental health attendant was Jesus. As I am writing this now, I can see why I thought she was Jesus. She was black with long dark dreads, tall and slender.

When I was in the hospital for the second time, a few people came to see me outside of Stacey, and that was ok. Though I was getting better, I was in a depressive state. When I was at my lowest point, I received a call from my cousin Julie who was a Christian. She had a prophetic word from the Lord for me. The call from Julie ultimately changed my life. I knew the words Julie spoke to me were from God because the stuff she said to me, nobody could have known, but God! At the end of the conversation, Julie asked me if I wanted to give my life to Christ. She told me to think about it. I thought about the conversation a lot. I did not know it at the time, but the love of God was drawing me to salvation, His saving grace!

I told Stacey about the conversation. She was interested as well. Julie led us both in a simple prayer of repentance (forgiveness) of our sins. We were born again! Bless God! My new journey in life had begun. I was not perfect, but I was forgiven. There were many things about my new life I had to learn. My life changed in ways I did not understand, but I was on a new journey, a journey my life needed so badly.

Chapter 10

Living My Best Life

I remember this day so well...It was late October, around Halloween. Stacy and I met and helped another lesbian couple who needed assistance for children. When we returned to the apartment one of Stacy's friends came over. I don't recall the individual's name. As I was going inside, Stacy hit me on my butt. I felt disrespected and disgusted by Stacy. I was upset. I talked to my cousin Julie. She was supportive. Cousin Julie encouraged me to get a bible. I followed her advice and purchased a bible. The entire landscape of my life was changing. Shortly after accepting Christ as my Lord and Savior, Stacy left me. When I was at work, she packed up her things and exited the building. The apartment was void of her and her belongings. I tried to call her, but she did not answer. I was kind of lost, but I was ok.

I began reading the bible and spending time with God. I created an atmosphere of worship at home with music a friend gave me.

I threw away the stuff I collected from my relationship with Stacy. I was creating a space in my life for something more than what I had experienced. Thinking back, I loved that apartment, it was the place of my personal transformation! My focus was working, taking care of my daughter, Layla, and personal fitness. I was working out heavy in the gym.

Chapter 11

The Church

My cousin invited me to her church. I accepted the invitation, but before I went to church, I met up and hung out with a girl who liked me. The Church, Liberty Christian Outreach Ministry under the leadership of the late Bishop Billy K. Bamberg was different from any other church. I was searching for God. I did not know what to do. I did not know much about the bible, but the church made a lasting impression.

Financially, it was challenging with one income. I had just enough money for my bills, but I bought a dress from Walmart for church. It was Sunday morning; I was in church because I wanted to be there! I did not know it at the time, but God had me! He was providing for me! I told my cousin Julie about my financial struggle. She and her husband blessed me with money to put gas in my car. I was so grateful for their kindness and God's provision!

Chapter 12

My Mind

Despite my new life in Christ, I continued to experience mental battles that triggered manic, impulsive behaviors. My mind began to rebel against me again with psychotic episodes. I returned to the mental hospital several times for treatment. I did not know what was going on mentally, but I continued to press my way to church every time I was attacked mentally. It was a serious battle in my mind. I was hearing and seeing things that were not real, but in my manic world, the images were alive and real.

During a manic episode, every thought and action is amplified. I started studying and taking notes at an exuberant speed. I wrote everything I heard the preacher say and more. My mind was experiencing battles I had no control over, so I thought. Several people told me I did not need to take medication, but I made the best decision to start taking my medications as prescribed.

Though I gave it my best effort, it was a challenge to keep up with the pill dosages. In 2016, I started taking injections.

Eventually, I found a medication, invega trinza in the highest dosage agreed with my body. I was making substantial progress. I was no longer hearing voices or hallucinating. I was fully aware of my surroundings. My mental health was improving, but my doctor wanted to wean me off the medication. At that point, I was tired of my doctor's trial and error approach to my treatment.

I continued taking the invega trinza. It was expensive, but God always made a way for me out of no way to get the help I needed. I was my own advocate. I put in the work to get what was necessary for healing. My healing process was top priority. I started to experience good results from my healing.

I was not sure if God was ready for me to go back to work and school, but I did. I did not want to stay home and do nothing. I wanted to have money to get the things I desired for my daughter Layla and myself. My mind was clear. My emotions were stable. I was healing. My daughter had a mother who was healing. We were both healing!

Chapter 13

The Fall

Though I no longer had same sex attraction, I engaged in a heterosexual relationship or situationship with a guy who liked me from high school. I started spending time with him and neglecting my responsibilities. At the time, I was having sexual relations with him. I did not know as a single Christian woman it was my responsibility to pursue purity and not engage in sexual intimacy outside of marriage.

While I dated him, I continued going to church. I went to a church service in my hometown. My friend's brother was the speaker for the evening. He preached about distractions. His words about distractions kept ringing in my head. I did not understand what distractions meant and how it could negatively affect my life. In time, I learned a distraction is anything the enemy uses to get you off track with God and the plans He has for your life. It is the enemy's job to persuade you to sin against God.

Distractions are always something or someone that you conform to or accept. Distraction may look good, feel good or act good, but distractions are not good for you! I was blind to the truth; the guy I was dating was a distraction! I was not reading my bible as much. My worship music became silent. I spent most of my time with him. I was sinking deeper and deeper into sin. I started to notice his behaviour. He was deceitful and manipulative.

The thing I dreaded happened; I missed my period. I was in panic mode. I did not want to have a baby with birth defects because of the medication I was taking. I did not want to be someone else's baby momma. I took several pregnancy tests. They were all positive. I told my pastor I was pregnant. Because of my actions, I had to step down from my role as an usher.

As I sat in service on the second row, I remember Bishop Bamberg preaching about a lady who was sleeping around. All I could remember was him saying, "sleeping with the enemy." I was squirming in my seat the whole service. I was convicted about my actions. Conviction is the Lord's way of correcting and convincing you that what you are doing is in error and sinning against Him.

I told the guy who I was dating at the time I was pregnant. He had the nerve to accuse me of sleeping around. The truth prevailed. He was the one sleeping around. I could tell by his actions.

My suspicions about him were confirmed by his Facebook page. He had just gotten out of a situationship and into another right after I left him alone. I ended the relationship. God rescued me from destruction! He provided a way of escape! I took another pregnancy test. It was negative! I was not pregnant! I repented, asking the Lord to forgive me. He is faithful and just to forgive us of our sins when we ask for forgiveness. He cleanses us from all unrighteousness, John 1:9 KJV.

However, that did not stop me fully from trying to have sexual encounters, but God was faithful then and He is faithful now to the success of my life. Being a Christian does not mean you are perfect, being a Christian means you are forgiven. As my pastor would say, "where there is sin, grace much more abounds, Romans 5:20. I did not condemn myself because there is no condemnation in Christ Jesus, Romans 8:1.

Chapter 14

Redemption

After all I have said, I want to leave you with this: Though my life has been chaotic and traumatic, God has always been with me. He never left nor abandoned me, Deuteronomy 31:6. The best thing I have ever done is release the reigns of my life to God. I surrendered. I gave Him total control of my life! In return: I am happy. I have joy. I Am restored. I Am redeemed. I have peace. I have an abundant life in Christ Jesus. I do not have a desire to go back to the life I once lived which was an Interrupted Life.

I needed redemption! I was always searching for a pure unconditional love that no man or woman could give. I was restless, looking for love in all the wrong places and too many faces.

In all of my life lessons, I can give advice telling you what to and what not to do, but I will rest with this one plea as stated in Romans 10:9-10 NLT; "[9] If you openly declare that Jesus is Lord and believe in your heart that God raised him from the dead, you will be saved. [10] For it is by believing in your heart that you are made right with God, and it is by openly declaring your faith that you are saved.

If you believed and made the Romans 10:9 confession, Welcome Home to the Family of God, you have been reunited to God the Father, through His Son Jesus Christ! Amen!

A symbol of hope and redemption

Hawaiian Hibiscus

After Thoughts

Empris...a Genesis Creation

created in His Image wonderfully, fearfully, masterfully
Genesis 1:27
Psalm 139:13,14

Let others praise you...

I truly enjoyed reading Interrupted My Redeemed Life: A Memoir. As I began reading, it immediately caught my attention. Every chapter grabbed me. This was a great testimony from Empris V. Jones, that young and old need to read. It was filled with detail, honesty, and truth. God was so amazing, through it all. He gets all the Glory and the Praise! He has no respectable person; He will get the Glory out our lives.

Terri H.
Debut Author
Mastering the Storm

What a story! Your book and life story are amazing, interesting, and very redemptive! With a life like yours, you should consider/pray about possibly doing something with Christian Counselling. Your story could be the story someone needs to hear. Your life story could be a ministry to many different groups of people.

Rachel M.
Preschool/Early Childhood
Assistant Teacher

MY! MY! MY! WHAT A STORY! This young lady's testimony proves that we don't have to give up, NO MATTER WHAT the circumstances. As I was reading her manuscript, I cried and rejoiced while seeing the hand of God on her life from a child to an adult. Her story is both inspiring and soul searching. I pray that Empris will one day have counselling sessions as well as speaking engagements. So many people need to know: WITH GOD ALL THINGS ARE POSSIBLE!

Wanda T.
Debut Author
Stop Skipping the Pages of Life

About the book, Interrupted, it was amazing and exciting! As I began reading, I couldn't put it down. Though the author's life was hard and challenging, life bounced her around, she never gave up. In the end when she found the Lord, her life changed because there's no way that you can come in contact with Jesus and still remain the same!

Esther G.
Gospel Recording Artist
Debut Author

As I read this extraordinary book, I didn't know what to expect when I began reading. I wasn't expecting such honesty from the writer. Her words were excitingly honest! She has a message that touched me profoundly. I am extremely proud of her for having the courage to share her story with the world. God had a plan and a purpose for her life, and she is walking in it!

Lola W.
Christian Life Coach, Hiscoach
Debut Author

I Am Redeemed, Empris V. Jones!

Order your copy @
www.EprisVJones.com
Amazon
and other select online platforms

Made in the USA
Middletown, DE
10 December 2025

22964209R00029